AROMATHERAPY

A helpful guide to the use of holistic aromatherapy for harmony and well-being

Edited by
JAN KUSMIREK

THE INSTITUTE OF CLASSICAL AROMATHERAPY
The Fragrant Studies "Pilgrim Centre"
Orchard Court, Magdalene Street,
Glastonbury, Somerset, U.K. BA6 9EW

CONTENTS

INTRODUCTION

Aromatherapy is gaining increasing popularity in Britain today, and not only within the field of complementary and natural medicines; its benefits are beginning to be recognised within the orthodox medical and particularly the nursing professions.

This booklet has been compiled together with the Institute of Classical Aromatherapy to help the home user make the most of the essential oils used in Aromatherapy. It is not intended to be a comprehensive guide to the practice of Aromatherapy, which requires a thorough professional training. Nor should this publication be regarded as a substitute for expert advice. For serious medical symptoms, you should always consult a qualified medical or complementary practitioner.

However, used correctly, essential oils can be used safely by your family and friends at home as an invaluable aid to relaxation, stress relief, beauty care, and to the improvement of health and well being.

Within complementary medicine, Aromatherapy is an ever-expanding field. There are a number of different training schools, each with its own particular emphasis. The information given here has been compiled from several different sources. It is intended for general interest and may not represent the views, policy or practice of the Institute of Classical Aromatherapy.

WHAT IS AROMATHERAPY?

Aromatherapy is a natural treatment which uses the concentrated herbal energies in essential oils from plants in association with massage, friction, inhalation, compresses and baths. An enjoyable experience in itself, it also improves and maintains well-being, health and beauty.

While many massage practitioners and relaxation experts use essential oils as an adjunct to their work, Aromatherapy is a holistic treatment in its own right. In the hands of qualified practitioners it can help to combat a wide range of physical and emotional problems. It has been shown to be successful not only in the treatment of stress-related conditions but also with muscular, circulatory, respiratory, digestive and skin problems and ailments. And, as this booklet describes, it can be used at home for relaxation, health and beauty care, as an adjunct to other treatment in illness, for first aid, or simply to enhance the atmosphere at home or work.

Aromatherapy is a holistic form of healing which works with the body to promote health. Like other forms of holistic treatment, such as homoeopathy, Classical Aromatherapy does not work on the 'magic bullet' principle favoured by orthodox medicine, in which one chemical or drug is aimed at a specific disease. In fact, all essential oils have a wide range of applications.

If you visit a qualified Aromatherapist, he or she will first discover not only what your symptoms are, but what kind of person you are. You will be asked about your diet, lifestyle, and any stresses and strains in your life. Only then will the practitioner decide which oil or combination of oils will suit you best, and the choice may change from visit to visit as your well-being improves. Massage with the oils forms a major part of the treatment, but the Aromatherapist may also act as counsellor, and advise on nutrition, exercise, and other aspects of your health.

AROMAS, HERBS AND OILS THROUGH HISTORY

The use of aromatic materials for healing is as old as time. The medicinal properties of scented plants, flowers and woods were known to all the great ancient civilisations including Egypt, Babylon, China, India, Arabia, Greece and Rome.

The priest-physicians of ancient Egypt used fragrances that we know today, such as Cedar oil, in medicine, embalming, and in religious ceremonies. The ancient Greeks, who believed that perfumes were formulated by the gods, used aromatic medicines and cosmetics, while the Romans used fragrant oils in massage. The word 'perfume' itself derives from the Latin par fumare, meaning 'through smoke'.

In many oriental cultures, the aromatic smoke of burning herbs had and still has religious and spiritual connotations, representing the prayers of worshippers and aiding the journey of the departing spirit at funerals. Scented herbs, oils and incense have also long been used in the Far East for both religious and medicinal purposes, while American Indians burn aromatic herbs to create smoke for their healing ceremonies.

Perfume and ointment makers have been involved for centuries in healing and promoting well-being. The Arabs, who specialised in using fragrant and aromatic substances, rediscovered the art of distilling and were among the first to use essential oils as we know them today.

In the West, the term 'essential oils' was coined by the 16th-century alchemists who were pursuing the 'quintessence', or secret of life; the ancient philosophers believed that there was a quintessential, or fifth, element, which formed heavenly bodies and pervaded all things. Later, the name was shortened to essential oils or essences. In 16th-century Germany a physician called Jerome of Brunswick documented 25 essential oils, all still in use today.

In the late 17th century, when herbs were used to combat pestilence and disease, herbalists like the famous Nicholas Culpeper used essential oils including Peppermint in their medicines; in times of plague, people carried pomanders made with oranges and cloves to mask unpleasant smells and ward off infection.

Until the early part of this century, all perfumes and many medicines relied on essential oils; then cheaper synthetic and chemical flavourings and scents began to take over. Nonetheless, the finest perfume and soap manufacturers have continued to use essential oils to give luxury products that quality which no imitation can match.

The revival of interest in essential oils began in the 1930s, with the French chemist Rene Gatefossé. He was working in the laboratory of his family's perfume business, when he burnt his hand badly. He plunged it into the nearest available liquid, which happened to be a bowl of neat lavender oil. Not only did the burn heal astonishingly quickly, but there was no scarring. Impressed, Gatefossé began to research the healing properties of other essential oils, and published his book *Aromatherapie* in 1937.

In World War II the interest in Aromatherapy was pursued in France by Dr Jean Valnet, a medical doctor, who successfully used essential oils as internal treatment for wounded soldiers. At the same time, an Austrian biochemist, Marguerite Maury, was developing the use of essential oils with massage techniques.

During this period the development of antibiotics and chemical antiseptics pushed the use of these powerful, natural oils into the background. Today, however, many people are disillusioned with synthetic, chemical ingredients in food, medicine, cosmetics and so on, and we are witnessing a marked turning towards healing methods that are natural, safe, and enjoyable.

In Britain, Aromatherapy has continued to be developed both by the orthodox medical profession as well as those in alternative and complementary practice. Numbers of nurses have trained in Aromatherapy and it is not that uncommon to find Aromatherapy being offered in orthodox medical centres. Research studies in Europe, Australia and the United States among other countries, show that essential oils used in Aromatherapy have definite therapeutic properties.

WHAT ARE ESSENTIAL OILS?

Most of us are already familiar with essential oils in everyday life, probably without realising it. Each time we add spice to a recipe, put mint sauce on roast lamb or crush a clove of garlic for a salad dressing, we are using essential oils. Many sweets are flavoured with essential oils or their derivatives; some liqueurs rely on them for the characteristic flavours, including aniseed and caraway.

Essential oils, or 'essences', are the most potent form of a plant's aromatic and fragrant materials. They are obtained, usually by distillation, from the flowers, leaves, stems, bark or wood of aromatic plants and trees. For example, for Chamomile oil the flower heads are used; for Lemon, the zest of the rind. Peppermint is made using the whole herb, and Sandalwood using the heartwood of the tree. Often huge amounts of raw material are needed to produce just a few drops of essential oil.

Essential oils are not oils in the everyday sense; they are not greasy or fatty. They are volatile, highly concentrated and extremely complex substances, which evaporate quickly leaving little or no stain. Individual essential oils may contain many hundreds of chemical components, some in infinitesimal quantities, which all react together in a way impossible to reproduce synthetically. Essential oils are far more than pleasant-smelling perfume oils: they have specific actions, many of them medicinal. All of them are to some degree antiseptic, some (such as Tea Tree) quite powerfully so; some are also anti-viral and antibiotic, and so can help to combat infections. Others are anti-inflammatory and can relieve both external burns and inflammatory conditions. Many are very useful in helping to stimulate the body's immune defence system and can be used not only for convalescence but also preventatively. Many are detoxifying and can help to clear congestion in the organs and lymphatic system.

Unlike drugs, some essential oils are particularly good at harmonising states of imbalance. Thus, when you read the descriptions of the individual oils, you will see that some have both a tonic and sedative action, according to the state of the user. Also unlike drugs, many of the essential oils listed in this booklet have similar or overlapping properties. Thus you may find different properties for the same oils listed in different books.

HOW THEY WORK WITH BODY AND MIND

The newly expanding field of complementary and holistic medicine recognises the importance of the link between mind and body; that is, our emotional response to external stress has a direct effect on the body. How stresses affect us depends on our own constitution; some people may respond with ulcers or digestive upsets, some with anxiety and insomnia, while others may develop high blood pressure. Holistic medicine takes into account the difference in symptoms and the individual stresses underlying them.

Essential oils appear to work on all levels. In massage, their physical properties penetrate the skin and reach the bloodstream in infinitesimal quantities to heal our muscles and organs. At the same time we are receiving their scents through the nose, whether through massage or other applications. It appears that they can activate a deep part of the brain, which stores memories, and that they also have an effect on the nervous system so that they can help to reduce anxiety, for instance – without the side effects of chemical tranquillisers.

THE IMPORTANCE OF QUALITY

To gain the best results only the best quality oils should be used, and they should be bought from a reputable source. Some oils are easier to obtain than others, so they vary in price; the rarest oils can be quite expensive. However, Aromatherapy is one area in which you really do get what you pay for; very cheap oils may be adulterated and offer little in the way of aroma. Since quality oils are highly concentrated, a small bottle goes a long way.

A good essential oil will come from a named botanic species and the aroma will be vigorous and lively, rather than simply strong. The extra sparkle and vitality of a top quality oil is always obvious in comparison with inferior oils.

Sometimes cheaper oils are added to more expensive ones, or oils are 'extended' by adding alcohol or a vegetable oil; these will produce a cheaper product, but will not give the real benefits of the essential oils used in Classical Aromatherapy.

Organic Oils, because of their absolute purity, are usually the best. They may come from naturally growing wild plants, or from wild crafted crops whose seeds have been sown in areas where the plant grows naturally. Other oils come from systems of biological or organic farming, and are often referred to as 'natural' rather than organic.

The best quality Lavender oil, for example, is grown at a height above 3,000 feet and contains a high level of the chemical Linalyl acetate which produces the most relaxing oil. But much of the lavender used in poorer commercial essential oils is grown much closer to sea level.

The aroma of the best oils varies naturally from year to year because of changes in climate, rainfall and soil conditions. So oils that smell exactly the same year after year are likely to have been altered in some artificial way to ensure a consistent aroma.

Carrier oils: Essential oils are highly concentrated and as a rule should not be applied neat. For massage, Aromatherapists blend them with vegetable oils called 'carrier oils'. The best carrier oils are virgin cold-pressed oils which contain active vitamins and fatty acids; they do not have a powerful aroma of their own. Those used by Aromatherapists include Sweet Almond, Walnut, Wheatgerm, Grapeseed, Jojoba, Apricot Kernel and Hazelnut. It is also possible, and preferable, to buy carrier oils specially pre-blended for the purpose.

Ready-blended oils can be bought ready mixed in a carrier oil, made up for specific purposes such as relaxation, baths, massaging aching muscles, and so on. Again, watch out for quality. A good quality pre-mixed, subtly fragrant oil can be very effective, and provides a good introduction to the use of essential oils.

STORING OILS

Always keep oils in the dark bottles in which they are supplied, in a cool, dry place, away from any substances, such as homoeopathic medicines, which might be affected by the aroma. Keep the caps tightly closed to avoid evaporation.

When you make up your own blends, also store them in dark glass bottles (never plastic), and keep the caps tightly screwed on. They should keep for three months, stored in a cool place.

USING ESSENTIAL OILS AT HOME

Qualified Aromatherapists use essential oils to treat a surprising number of ailments. Since this booklet is intended for non-professional use, included are the main uses of a selection of oils which can be safely used at home, for yourself, family and friends.

While serious conditions should be treated by a qualified practitioner, many common ailments can be relieved safely and effectively at home with Aromatherapy. You may soon come to regard essential oils as a vital part of your home first aid kit.

For self-help, essential oils are most commonly used to relieve aches and pains, for relaxation and stress reduction, and for skin and hair care, but they have much wider possibilities.

Many oils have proven antiseptic properties and can be used as first aid and ongoing treatment for cuts, burns, insect bites and bruises. Others are anti-inflammatory, anti-bacterial, antibiotic, etc. Oils with anti-fungal properties can be used in such conditions as athlete's foot and other fungal infections. Some can be used as an aid in the overall management of more serious conditions such as candida, arthritis and rheumatism.

In addition, since the oils work through the brain to act on the emotions, they are very useful not only for stress-relief, but in cases of anxiety, overwork, stage fright, etc.

Lists of oils recommended for specific physical and emotional symptoms are given on pages 19–32. While essential oils may help to alleviate symptoms, people suffering from serious conditions should always seek expert advice from a qualified Aromatherapist.

Caution should be exercised when using the oils to treat children, in pregnancy, etc., and there are some people for whom Aromatherapy is not always suitable. So do take time to read the Cautions section on pages 17–18; if in doubt, seek advice from a qualified practitioner.

SELECTING OILS

If you want to alleviate a specific problem, first look up your symptoms in the list of Physical Symptoms, on pages 19–27 and see which oils are recommended;

then, if appropriate, read the list of Mental/Emotional Symptoms, pages 28–32. For example, if you are suffering from fatigue, are your symptoms accompanied by anxiety or depression, or caused by overwork? To complete the picture, read the descriptions of the recommended oils on pages 33–55. Then you can make up a blend of the two or three oils which come closest to your personal needs.

Since we are all individuals, some oils will be more appropriate to particular people than others. Enjoy experimenting with the oils; experience will help you to become more expert.

The sniff test: If you can, sniff essential oils before using them to make sure that they appeal to your sense of smell as well as fitting your other needs. Essential oils have a powerful aroma which can cause a strong reaction when you sniff them, especially if you sniff direct from an open bottle. The best way to test the scent of an oil is to put a single drop onto a handkerchief, and then gently inhale from that.

BLENDING OILS

The concept of individuality is important in Aromatherapy, and it is rare for two people to react in exactly the same way. We can, however, generalise about the effects of particular essential oils which have specific actions – for example, a particular group of plants may have anti-inflammatory properties, some are relaxing and sedative, some invigorating and so on. Blends of 2–3 oils can be made with these general characteristics to suit your personal needs.

Your chosen oils can be blended together and diluted in a carrier oil, but do not exceed the total amounts recommended.

Oils bought ready blended in a carrier oil for general purposes, like baths, massage and room fragrance, will not require further dilution.

USING THE OILS

Once you have chosen a suitable oil or blend of oils, you can use them in the following ways:

Massage

Massage is a very effective way to relieve stress and tension. The ideal of course is to visit a professional Aromatherapist. However, for home care, massaging yourself or getting a partner to give you a gentle massage will still have benefits. Massage encourages circulation and eases minor aches and pains; it enables the essential oils to be absorbed and used by the skin and body. You do not have to have a full body massage to benefit; you can rub the blended oils locally into the area giving problems, whether it be muscular aches and pains, a stiff neck or a bronchitic chest. In self-massage, use gentle strokes towards the heart, to encourage the circulation. When massaging the abdomen, move your hands in clockwise circles, following the flow of the intestines; among other benefits, this helps to relieve constipation.

Making up Massage Oils

Choose a vegetable based carrier oil, preferably a blend of two or three oils with therapeutic properties of their own. Add 2 drops of your chosen essential oil/s to 5ml (1 tsp) of carrier oil. Keep in a dark, stoppered glass bottle, and always recap tightly after use. The aroma will be taken up over a period of time, so the oil will smell more rounded after a week than just after it has been mixed.

Most oils are suitable for massage; for specific problems, see the lists of symptoms. Bear in mind that some oils are relaxing and some stimulating.

Examples of recommended blends are:

For relaxation – Geranium and Lavender

For aches and pains – Juniper, Lemon and Rosemary

For cellulitis – Juniper, Geranium and Rosemary

Baths

Bathing with essential oils is not just a pleasant way to relax; it can help to relieve many aches and pains and other physical conditions. Use a ready-mixed blend, or add a maximum of 7–8 drops of pure oil to your bath, ideally at about 30°C, just before getting in. Stir the water well to disperse the oils. Do not use any other bath oil, salts or foam preparations at the same time. Close the windows and doors and relax in the water for ten minutes. You will benefit from the action of both the oil on your skin and in the water vapour.

Most oils are suitable for baths; however some of the stronger aromas, like Peppermint, may cause skin irritation. Check the recommended uses of the oils.

For children use 2 drops of oil to a bath.

Footbaths

Add up to 5 drops of oil to a bowl of hand-hot water and soak the feet for ten minutes. Particularly suitable for tired and perspiring feet are Cypress, Juniper, Lemon and Tea Tree.

Sauna

Stir 3 or 4 drops of your chosen oil/s in water and then splash on the hot stones.

Inhalation/Facial Steaming

This way of using oils simultaneously gives your skin a cleansing treat while helping to clear congested lungs and sinuses, catarrh and sore throats.

On average use 2–3 drops to 1 pint of water. Float the oil on the surface of a bowl of steaming water, just off the boil. Drape a bath towel over your head and breathe in the steam for 2–3 minutes.

For nasal congestion, breathe through the nose; for a sore throat breathe through the mouth. Do not persist if this causes discomfort.

Exercise caution if you suffer from allergic conditions such as hayfever and asthma.

Compresses

Use *hot compresses* for long-standing conditions like backache, arthritis and rheumatic pain.

Use *cold compresses* for recent injuries or acute conditions such as sprains, headaches, bruises and swelling.

For hot compresses, use water as hot as you can comfortably handle; for cold compresses, add ice to cold water. Add to the water up to 6 drops of essential oil or 3 for small areas like the forehead, fold a face cloth and place it on the surface of the water so that it takes up the essential oil. Wring out, and apply where needed (avoid getting into eyes).

Hair and Face Oil

Some oils are particularly good for the skin and hair (see list of Physical Symptoms). Use proportions of 1 drop of essential oil to 10ml (2 tsp) carrier oil (preferably pre-blended for the purpose) for a pre-bath facial oil or as an after-bath body lotion and moisturiser.

For hair conditioning, massage the blend into the scalp and leave for 15–30 minutes before shampooing.

Headlice can be successfully and pleasantly treated with a mixture of Eucalyptus or Tea Tree with Lavender and Rosemary, using 40 drops of essential oils to 100ml carrier oil. Apply to wet hair, massage well in and leave for an hour before shampooing and combing out with a fine-toothed comb. Repeat as necessary.

Hair Rinse

After washing your hair, stir 1 drop of oil in the water in which you give your hair its final rinse. Or make up a hair rinse as follows:

4 drops essential oil to 1 litre water. Use a screw top bottle and shake well to disperse the oil each time you use it, as it does not dissolve in water.

Suitable oils for hair include Rosemary, Geranium and Rosewood for dark hair, Chamomile and Lemon for fair hair.

Skin Lotion

Skin lotions/tonics can be made by adding 10 drops essential oil to 50ml of spring water. Use a screw top bottle and shake well to disperse. Suitable oils are listed under 'Skin' in the list of symptoms, page 26.

Mouthwash

Using a screw topped bottle, mix 2 drops oil with 285ml/½ pint spring water, shaking well to disperse the oil each time you use it.

For fresh breath, suitable oils include Peppermint and Lemon. For mouth infections and gum problems, use Tea Tree. Don't swallow the mouthwash.

Room Fragrance

Used as room fragrance, essential oils create a pleasant atmosphere; at the same time, specific oils will have an effect on your mood, creating a good ambience for meditation, work, relaxation, romance or sleep. Some will also help to fumigate the air in cases of infectious illness. There are several methods of using oils for room fragrance:

Add a few drops of essential oil to a bowl of dried flowers or pot pourri.

Add a few drops to drawer liners and padded clothes hangers.

Put a couple of drops on a hot light bulb.

Add a few drops to a ball of cotton wool and tuck it behind a warm radiator, or float 2 drops on a saucer of water near a warm radiator. Oil vaporisers are available today in a number of shops. Float a couple of drops of oil on water at the top of a bowl, and burn a night light underneath, to release the aroma into the air.

Most oils can be used for room fragrance. Some are particularly suitable for special purposes, including:

Meditation: Cedarwood and Sandalwood.

Infection: Peppermint (alone); Tea Tree (alone); Eucalyptus and Rosemary; Lavender and Lemon.

Romance: Ylang Ylang, Geranium, Sandalwood.

Relaxation/Sleep: Chamomile, Lavender, Sandalwood, Ylang Ylang.

On Handkerchiefs/Tissues

For colds, headaches, stuffiness, travel sickness, etc. put a drop or two on a handkerchief to sniff at intervals.

As an aid to sleep, put 1–2 drops on a handkerchief or tissue and place beside your bed or close to your pillow. You can put drops direct on the pillow, but do not let your skin come into contact with the neat oil.

Neat Application

As a general rule, do not apply neat oils to the skin as they can produce a skin reaction. However, for the relief of insect bites and stings, and to disinfect cuts, a drop or two of certain oils (e.g. Tea Tree, Lavender or Rosewood) can be used on the spot. Put 1–2 drops on cotton wool, and dab gently.

SPECIAL USES

The hectic pace of life today makes particular demands on everyone. Women often have to combine work, home care and the demands of children. Modern life exacts an emotional toll on men, too, while they also engage in types of work and sports that can place great demands on the body.

Aromatherapy can really help to redress the balance by soothing away the effects of a strenuous day, boosting self-confidence and inner strength.

For women, especially feminine oils are: Clary Sage, Geranium, Lavender, Marjoram, Ylang Ylang.

For men, especially masculine oils are: Cypress, Frankincense, Lemon, Rosewood and oils with a dual aspect like Clary Sage and Geranium.

Essential oils that help to refresh and uplift are: Lavender, Lemon, Rosemary, Rosewood. Essential oils that help you to feel warm and secure are: Chamomile, Clary Sage, Lavender, Orange, Ylang Ylang.

CAUTIONS

Essential oils are powerful, and should be used with care. In using the oils at home, follow the guidelines below:

- Aromatherapy can be very helpful during pregnancy and labour, but only under qualified guidance. If you are pregnant, you are strongly recommended to consult a qualified Aromatherapist.

- Some oils are stimulants, which may sometimes affect people suffering from epilepsy. Sufferers should seek medical advice before using essential oils.

- For babies and small children use in extra-dilute quantities.

- Keep bottles out of reach of small children.

- Unless specifically indicated, do not apply neat oils direct on to the skin, as they can cause irritation.

- For the same reason, it is advisable to give yourself a patch test on a small area of skin when using your own blend. Note that certain drugs, stress, and the menstrual cycle can also affect your sensitivity.

- Keep oils away from the eyes, and don't rub your eyes after handling them. If you should get any in your eyes, wash them out with plenty of fresh water; seek medical advice if necessary.

- Essential oils are flammable, so do not put them on or near a naked flame.

- Some are solvents and may damage certain plastics and polished wood surfaces.

- Never take the oils by mouth, unless under medical instructions.

- If you are taking homoeopathic remedies, check with your practitioner before using essential oils, as it is believed that strong aromas can cancel the effects of homoeopathic medicine.

- If you suffer from skin or other allergies, use the oils very carefully, and patch-test before using widely. If you are unfortunate enough to have an allergic reaction to perfume you are likely to be allergic to all essential oils. In this case, seek some other gentle form of therapy, such as Homoeopathy or the Bach Flower Remedies.

- If in any doubt at all, consult a qualified Aromatherapist.
  (See the addresses of organisations on page 56.)

INDEX OF PHYSICAL SYMPTOMS

N.B. These lists have been compiled from several sources.

Before using essential oils, read the Cautions on pages 17–18.

If you are suffering from serious medical symptoms,

or if in any doubt, consult a qualified practitioner.

**Most widely recommended.*

SYMPTOM	RECOMMENDED OILS	HOW TO USE
Abscess. external	Lavender, Tea Tree	Dab with 1–2 drops on cotton wool
• weeping	Frankincense	
Aches and pains	*(See Muscular aches and pains)*	
Acne	*(See under Skin)*	
Addictions	Clary Sage	Bath; massage; room fragrance/diffuser
Ageing, problems of	Rosewood *(See also Menopause)*	Bath; massage; room fragrance/diffuser
Anaemia	Lemon	Bath; massage;
Appetite, loss of	Chamomile	Bath; massage;
Arthritis	Chamomile, Cypress, Juniper, Lavender, Lemon, Marjoram, Rosemary, Ginger	Bath; compress; massage/rub affected area with massage oil.
• swollen joints	Juniper	
Asthma	Cedarwood, Clary Sage, Eucalyptus, Lavender, Lemon, Marjoram	Bath; massage/rub with massage oil. Avoid inhalations
Athlete's foot	Lavender, Lemon, *Tea Tree	Footbath; dab with 1–2 drops on cotton wool
Backache	*(See Lumbar pain, Muscular aches and pains)*	
Baldness/Hair loss	Clary Sage, Lavender, *Rosemary, Ylang Ylang	Scalp oil
Bedwetting	Chamomile, Cypress, Lavender	Bath;massage
Bites,	*(See Insect bites)*	
Blisters	Lavender	Dab with 1–2 drops on cotton wool
Blood pressure **• high/low**	Clary Sage, *Lavender, Lemon, Marjoram, *Ylang Ylang, Rosemary	Bath; massage
Body odour	Clary Sage, Cypress, Juniper, Lemon, Rosewood	Bath; massage; skin lotion
Boils	Chamomile, Juniper, Lavender, Lemon, Tea Tree	Bath; compress; dab with 1–2 drops on cotton wool
Breath, bad	Lavender, Tea Tree	Mouthwash
Bronchitis	Cedarwood, Eucalyptus, Frankincense, Marjoram, Orange, Sandalwood Tangerine, *Tea Tree, Ginger	Bath; inhalation; massage/rub chest with massage oil

SYMPTOM	RECOMMENDED OILS	HOW TO USE
Bruises	*Lavender, Tea Tree	Bath; compress; dab with 1–2 drops on cotton wool
Burns	*Lavender, Chamomile, Eucalyptus, *Tea Tree	Bath; compress; for small burns apply neat
Candida albicans	Tea Tree	Bath; compress; massage
Catarrh	Cedarwood, Eucalyptus, Frankincense, Lavender, Lemon, Peppermint, Rosemary, Sandalwood, Tea Tree, Ginger	Bath; compress; inhalation
Cellulitis	Cypress, *Geranium, Juniper, Lavender, *Lemon, *Rosemary, Grapefruit, Patchouli	Bath; massage/rub with massage oil
Chilblains • itchy	Cypress, Juniper, Lavender, Lemon, Marjoram, Rosemary, Chamomile *(See also Circulation, poor)*	Bath; compress, footbath, dab with massage oil
Chilliness	Cypress, Frankincense, Marjoram, Rosemary	Bath; massage/rub with massage oil
Circulation, poor	Cypress, Juniper, Lemon, Marjoram, Orange, *Rosemary	Bath; massage/rub affected area with massage oil
Cold sores	Eucalyptus, Tea Tree	Dab with 1–2 drops on cotton wool
Colds • with sneezing	*Eucalyptus, Lavender, Lemon, Marjoram, Orange, Tangerine, *Tea Tree, Rosemary	Bath; massage/rub throat and chest with massage oil; inhalation; room fragrance/diffuser
Colic	Chamomile, Juniper, Lavender, Sandalwood	Bath; massage/rub abdomen with massage oil
Colitis	Rosemary	Bath; massage/rub affected area with massage oil
Constipation	*Rosemary, Marjoram, Peppermint, Orange, Tangerine, Ylang Ylang, Ginger	Bath; massage/rub abdomen clockwise with massage oil
Convalescence	Clary Sage	Bath; massage; room fragrance/diffuser
Corns	Lavender, *Lemon, Marjoram, Peppermint	Dab with 1–2 drops on cotton wool

SYMPTOM	RECOMMENDED OILS	HOW TO USE
Coughs	Cedarwood, Eucalyptus, Frankincense, Ginger, Lavender, Lemon, Marjoram, Sandalwood	Bath; inhalation; massage/rub throat and chest with massage oil; room fragrance/diffuser
• bronchitic	Cypress	
• dry	Cypress, Lavender, Sandalwood	
• spasmodic	Cypress	
Cramp	Clary Sage, Cypress, Juniper	Bath; massage/rub with massage oil
• after exercise	Rosemary, Marjoram	
Cuts	Eucalyptus, Lavender *Tea Tree	Compress; dab with 1–2 drops on cotton wool; a drop can be applied neat
Cystitis	Chamomile, Cedarwood, Cypress, Eucalyptus, Frankincense, *Juniper, *Lavender, *Sandalwood, *Tea Tree	Hot compress; massage/rub abdomen with massage oil
Dandruff	Cedarwood, Lavender, Rosemary, Tangerine	Hair oil; hair rinse
• with oily scalp	Cypress	
Dermatitis	*Chamomile, Geranium, Orange, Tangerine, *Tea Tree	Bath; compress; apply massage oil to affected area
Diarrhoea	Chamomile, Cypress, Eucalyptus, Geranium, Lavender, Peppermint, Rosemary, Sandalwood	Compress; massage
Earache	Chamomile, Lavender	Compress or cotton bud in ear with one drop of massage oil
Eczema	*Chamomile, Geranium, *Lavender, Patchouli, Sandalwood	Bath; apply massage oil to affected areas after patch-test (see Cautions pages 17–18)
• weeping	Juniper, Lavender	
Energy, lack of	Orange *(See also Exhaustion, Fatigue)*	Bath; massage; room fragrance/diffuser
Exhaustion	Clary Sage, Frankincense, Lavender	Bath; massage; room fragrance/diffuser
Fatigue	Geranium, Marjoram, Peppermint, Rosemary	Bath; massage; room fragrance/diffuser
Feet, sweaty	Cypress, Tea Tree	Bath; footbath
• deodorants for	Cypress, Juniper, Lemon	

SYMPTOM	RECOMMENDED OILS	HOW TO USE
Feet, tired	Peppermint	Footbath
Flatulence	Ginger, Grapefruit, Marjoram, Peppermint, Tangerine	Massage abdomen
Fluid retention	Eucalyptus, Geranium, *Juniper, Lavender, Rosemary, Sandalwood, Patchouli	Bath; massage
Frigidity	Clary Sage, Rosewood, Sandalwood, *Ylang Ylang	Bath; massage; room fragrance/diffuser
Fungal infections	Geranium, *Tea Tree	Bath; compress; dab with 1–2 drops on cotton wool
Gastritis	Lavender, Peppermint, Tea Tree	Bath; massage/rub abdomen with massage oil
Gum infections	Tea Tree, Cypress	Mouthwash
Haemorrhoids (piles)	*Cypress, Frankincense, Juniper	Bath; general massage
Hair care:	Chamomile, Rosemary	Hair rinse; hair oil
• dry	Geranium, Lavender, Sandalwood	
• oily/greasy	Clary Sage, Lemon *(See also Baldness, Dandruff, Headlice)*	
Hangover	Juniper, Rosemary	Bath; inhalation; massage
Hay fever	Juniper	Drops on handkerchief; rub massage oil on sinuses
Headache	Clary Sage, *Lavender, Rosemary, Marjoram, Peppermint	Bath; compress; inhalation; massage or apply oil to head, neck and shoulders
• congestive	Eucalyptus, Marjoram	
• with sinusitis	Eucalyptus	
• tension	Chamomile	
Headlice	Geranium, Lavender Tea Tree *(NB: Avoid getting oil in the eyes)*	Scalp oil
Hot flushes	Chamomile, Lavender	Bath; massage; room fragrance/diffuser
***Immune deficiency* (recurrent infections)**	Lavender, Lemon, Rosewood, Sandalwood, Tea Tree	Bath; massage; room fragrance/diffuser
Impotence	Clary Sage; Rosewood, Sandalwood, *Ylang Ylang	Bath; massage; room fragrance/diffuser

SYMPTOM	RECOMMENDED OILS	HOW TO USE
Indigestion	Chamomile, Juniper, Lemon, Peppermint, Orange, Sandalwood, Tangerine	Bath; massage/rub locally with massage oil
Infections	Tea Tree	Room fragrance/diffuser
Influenza	Cypress, Eucalyptus, Juniper, Lavender, Lemon, Peppermint, Tea Tree	Bath; inhalation, massage; room fragrance/diffuser
Insect bites/stings	Chamomile, Lavender, Lemon, Tea Tree	Apply one or two drops neat; bath; compress
Insomnia • when physically tired	Chamomile, *Lavender, Marjoram, Orange, Sandalwood, Tangerine, Ylang Ylang, Clary Sage *(See also under Mental/Emotional Symptoms for conditions causing the insomnia, e.g. Anxiety, Depression, etc.)*	Bath; massage; room fragrance; a drop or two on tissue beside pillow
Irritable bowel	Chamomile	Bath; massage abdomen
Joints: Painful • swollen See also Arthritis, Rheumatism	Lavender, Juniper, Rosemary Chamomile, Lavender	Bath; compress (cold for recent injury, hot for chronic pain); massage/rub affected area with massage oil
Laryngitis	Cypress, Lemon, Sandalwood	Bath; compress; inhalation; rub massage oil on throat and chest
Liver problems	Chamomile, Geranium, Juniper, Rosemary, Tangerine	Bath; massage/rub affected area with massage oil
Lumbar pain	Chamomile, Lavender, Rosemary	Bath; compress; massage/rub affected area with massage oil
Lymphatic congestion	*Rosemary, Geranium, Lavender	Bath; massage/rub with massage oil
Menopause	Chamomile, Clary Sage, Cypress, Geranium, Lavender, Sandalwood	Bath; inhalation; massage
Menstrual problems	*(See PMT, Periods)*	
Migraine	Chamomile, Clary Sage, *Lavender, *Marjoram, *Peppermint, Rosemary	Bath; massage head and neck; inhalation; room fragrance/diffuser
Mouth infections	Geranium, *Tea Tree	Mouthwash
Mouth ulcers • external	Lemon, *Tea Tree	Mouthwash Dab with 1–2 drops on cotton wool
Muscle spasm	Clary Sage	Rub with massage oil

SYMPTOM	RECOMMENDED OILS	HOW TO USE
Muscular aches and pains	Chamomile, Eucalyptus, Juniper, Lavender, Lemon, Marjoram, Peppermint, Ginger, Orange, Rosemary, Tangerine	Bath; compress; massage/rub affected area with massage oil
• after sport	Chamomile, Marjoram	
Nausea	Ginger, Grapefruit, Lavender, Peppermint, Rosewood	Bath; inhalation
Nettle rash	Chamomile, Tea Tree	Bath; compress; apply massage oil to affected area after patch-test (see Cautions, pages 17-18)
Neuralgia	Chamomile, Eucalyptus, Geranium, Lemon	Bath; compress; massage/rub affected area with massage oil
Nosebleed	Cypress, Frankincense, Lavender, Lemon	Compress
Periods		
• heavy	Cypress	Bath; compress; massage/rub abdomen with massage oil
• irregular	Chamomile, Clary Sage, Geranium, Lavender	
• painful	Chamomile, Clary Sage Cypress, Juniper, Rosemary	
• scanty	Juniper, Lavender	
Perspiration		
excessive	Clary Sage, Cypress	Bath; massage; skin lotion
Deodorants for,	*(See Body odour)*	
PMT (pre-menstrual tension)	Clary Sage, Chamomile, Geranium, Rosemary	Bath; compress; massage
• painful breasts	Geranium *(See also Fluid retention)*	
Psoriasis	Geranium, Juniper, Lavender, Tea Tree	Bath; compress; apply massage oil to affected area, after patch-test (see Cautions, pages 17-18)
Respiratory problems	Cedarwood, Eucalyptus, Frankincense, Peppermint, Rosemary, Sandalwood	Bath; compress; inhalation; massage/rub chest and throat with massage oil; room fragrance/diffuser
Rheumatism	Chamomile, Cypress, Juniper, Lavender, Marjoram, Lemon, Rosemary, Grapefruit, Ginger	Bath; compress; massage/rub affected area with massage oil
Sciatica	Eucalyptus, Juniper *(See also Muscular aches and pains, Rheumatism)*	Bath; compress; massage/rub affected area with massage oil

SYMPTOM	RECOMMENDED OILS	HOW TO USE
Sexual problems	Clary Sage, Rosewood, Sandalwood, *Ylang Ylang	Bath; massage; room fragrance/diffuser
Sinusitis	Eucalyptus, Lavender, Marjoram, Peppermint, Orange, Tea Tree	Bath; inhalation; compress; apply massage oil to sinus area
Skin care and problems:		
• **acne**	Cedarwood, Chamomile, Geranium, Grapefruit, Juniper, Lavender, Tea Tree, Patchouli	Bath; compress; massage; skin lotion
• **ageing/mature**	Clary Sage, Cypress, Frankincense, *Geranium, Lavender, Lemon, Orange, *Rosewood, *Sandalwood, Tangerine	
• **allergies**	Chamomile	
• **blackheads**	Peppermint	
• **blotchy**	Geranium	
• **broken veins**	Cypress, Lemon, Chamomile	
• **cracked**	Frankincense, Patchouli	
• **dry**	Geranium, Lavender, Orange, *Sandalwood, Tangerine	
• **greasy**	Lemon, Peppermint	
• **infections**	Tea Tree	
• **inflamed**	Chamomile, Clary Sage, Frankincense, Geranium, Lavender, Sandalwood, Tea Tree	
• **irritated/itchy**	Cedarwood, Chamomile, Lavender, Sandalwood	
• **oily**	Cedarwood, Cypress, Geranium, Juniper, Rosemary, Ylang Ylang	
• **sensitive**	Geranium	
	(See also Dermatitis, Eczema)	
Sprains	Chamomile, Lavender	Cold compress
Sunburn	Lavender	Bath; cold compress
Sweating, excessive	Cypress *(See also Body odour)*	Bath; massage

SYMPTOM	RECOMMENDED OILS	HOW TO USE
Throat		
• **burning**	Lavender	Bath; compress; rub massage oil on throat and upper chest
• **dry**	Lavender	
• **infections**	Clary Sage, Geranium, Sandalwood, *Tea Tree	
• **sore**	Clary Sage, Lavender, Lemon, Sandalwood Tea Tree	
Thrush	Tea Tree	Bath
Tinnitus	Lavender, Sandalwood	Compress
Toothache	Chamomile, Peppermint	Compress; mouthwash
Travel sickness	Ginger, Lavender, Peppermint	Sniff a drop or two on tissue
Urination		Bath; Massage/rub abdomen with massage oil
• **frequent**	Cypress	
• **painful**	Juniper, Lavender *(See also Cystitis)*	
Varicose veins	Cypress, Lemon, Patchouli	Bath; compress
Veruccas	Lemon, Tea Tree	Dab with neat oil
Warts	Lemon, Tea Tree	Dab with neat oil
Wounds	Lavender, Tea Tree	Bath; compress; can be applied neat

INDEX OF MENTAL/EMOTIONAL SYMPTOMS

N.B. This list has been compiled from several sources. For mental and emotional states, the appropriate oils can all be used in baths, inhalation, massage and room fragrance. A drop on a handkerchief or tissue can also be used.

MENTAL/EMOTIONAL SYMPTOMS	RECOMMENDED OILS
Absent-mindedness	Cedarwood
Ageing, feelings of	Tangerine
Anger	Chamomile, Peppermint, Ylang Ylang, Grapefruit
Anxiety	Cedarwood, Chamomile, Clary Sage, Frankincense, Geranium, Juniper, Lavender, Marjoram, Rosewood, Sandalwood, Tangerine
• sexual	Sandalwood, Ylang Ylang, Patchouli
Apathy	Lemon, Orange, Tangerine, Tea Tree
Bitterness	Lemon
Boredom	Orange
Burn-out	Frankincense
Change	
• coping with	Ylang Ylang
• difficulty in adjusting to	Clary Sage
• difficulty in making	Orange
Claustrophobia	Clary Sage, Frankincense
Compulsiveness	Clary Sage
Concentration, lack of	Cedarwood, Eucalyptus, Rosemary
Confidence, lack of	Ylang Ylang, Ginger
Confusion	Geranium, Lemon
Courage, lack of See also Fear	Frankincense
Critical of others	Rosewood
Cynicism	Sandalwood
Daydreaming	Cedarwood, Rosewood
Depression	Chamomile, Clary Sage, Frankincense, Geranium, Lavender, Orange, Sandalwood, Tangerine, Ylang Ylang
Despondency	Juniper
Detail, over-preoccupation with	Tea Tree
Discipline, Lack of	Frankincense
Disorientation	Rosemary
Dreams, recurrent	Clary Sage, Sandalwood
Empathy, lack of	Rosewood
Emptiness, emotional	Tangerine
Exhaustion, mental	Frankincense
• from overwork	Clary Sage, Orange

MENTAL/EMOTIONAL SYMPTOMS	RECOMMENDED OILS
Fatigue, mental	Frankincense, Lavender, Peppermint, Rosemary, Rosewood
Fear	Chamomile, Frankincense
• acute	Geranium
• of coming events	Sandalwood
• of confronting issues	Marjoram
• of the dark	Lavender
• of dying	Tangerine
• of effort	Sandalwood
• of failure	Lavender, Sandalwood, Ylang Ylang
• of going mad	Ylang Ylang
• of letting go	Ylang Ylang
• of people	Lavender, Ylang Ylang
• of others' opinions	Cypress
• rigid with	Geranium
• of showing feelings	Marjoram, Ylang Ylang
• with inner trembling	Lavender
• of unknown origin	Lavender
Frustration	Ylang Ylang
Giving in to others	Cypress
Grief	Marjoram
• for lost past	Tangerine
• prolonged after loss	Frankincense
Grudgingness	Lemon
Grumpiness	Rosewood
Guilt feelings	Juniper, Ylang Ylang
Hopelessness	Orange
Hostility	Clary Sage, Marjoram
Hyperactivity	Clary Sage, Lavender
Hypersensitivity	Peppermint
Hysteria	Chamomile, Lavender, Peppermint
Impatience	Chamomile, Lavender, Ylang Ylang
Impulsiveness	Chamomile
Indecision	Rosemary
Insecurity	Frankincense, Lavender, Sandalwood
Insomnia	Chamomile, Clary Sage, Lavender, Orange, Sandalwood, Tangerine, Ylang Ylang
Instability	Geranium, Rosewood
Irrationality	Lavender, Ylang Ylang

MENTAL/EMOTIONAL SYMPTOMS	RECOMMENDED OILS
Irritability	Chamomile, Cypress, Lavender, Marjoram, Sandalwood, Ylang Ylang
Jealousy	Cypress, Ylang Ylang
Joy, Lack of	Orange, Tangerine
Lethargy, listlessness	Clary Sage, Cypress, Juniper, Lemon, Orange, Rosemary, Sandalwood
Loneliness	Marjoram
Memory, poor	Rosemary
Moodiness, mood swings	Eucalyptus, Geranium, Lavender, Rosewood
Nerves:	
• exhausted	Chamomile, Clary Sage, Juniper, Lavender, Marjoram, Rosemary, Grapefruit
• living on	Chamomile *(See also Tension, nervous)*
Nightmares	Frankincense, Lavender
Nostalgia, living in past	Frankincense, Sandalwood, Tangerine
Obsession	Clary Sage, Sandalwood
• with past	Frankincense, Sandalwood
Obstinacy	Orange, Rosewood, Ylang Ylang
Overactive mind	Chamomile, Lavender, Marjoram
Overburdened	Rosewood
• by responsibilities	Rosemary
Over-emotional	Eucalyptus
Over-talkativeness	Cypress
Overwork	Lavender, Rosewood
• mental strain from	Clary Sage, Rosemary
Palpitations, nervous	Lavender
Panic attacks	Clary Sage, Frankincense, Lavender, Ylang Ylang
Paranoia	Frankincense, Lavender
Perseverance, lack of	Frankincense
Procrastination	Sandalwood, Ginger
Resentment	Clary Sage, Lemon, Sandalwood, Ylang Ylang
Resignation	Orange
Restlessness	Chamomile, Lavender
Rigidity, mental	Geranium, Rosewood

MENTAL/EMOTIONAL SYMPTOMS	RECOMMENDED OILS
Sadness	Marjoram, Orange
Selfishness, self-centredness	Lemon, Orange, Sandalwood
Self-criticism	Frankincense
Self-esteem, self-worth, lack of	Juniper, Rosemary, Sandalwood, Ylang Ylang
Sensitivity	Lemon, Sandalwood, Ylang Ylang
Shock	Tea Tree, Ylang Ylang
Shyness	Peppermint, Ylang Ylang
Stability, need for	Frankincense
Stage fright	Lavender
Strain, mental	Chamomile, Clary Sage, Marjoram, Rosemary
Stress, general	Cedarwood, Chamomile, Clary Sage Geranium, Juniper, Lavender, Marjoram, Tangerine, Grapefruit
Sulkiness	Clary Sage, Rosewood
Suspiciousness	Ylang Ylang
Tantrums in children	Chamomile
Tension, nervous	Cedarwood, Chamomile, Clary Sage, Cypress Frankincense, Geranium, Juniper, Lavender, Rosewood, Sandalwood, Tangerine, Ylang Ylang, Grapefruit
Thoughts	
• **gloomy**	Orange
• **irrational**	Marjoram
• **negative**	Clary Sage, Lavender
• **not in present**	Cedarwood, Patchouli
• **overactive**	Clary Sage, Lavender
• **over-analytical**	Clary Sage
• **racing**	Clary Sage
• **restless**	Chamomile
• **scattered**	Cedarwood
• **unclear**	Eucalyptus, Lemon, Juniper, Peppermint, Rosemary
Touchiness	Lemon
Uncleanness, feelings of	Tea Tree
Unforgivingness	Sandalwood
Unyielding to circumstances	Rosewood
Weak-willed	Cypress
Withdrawnness	Marjoram
Worry	Chamomile
• about future	Lavender, Sandalwood
• about past	Frankincense

TWENTY-TWO OILS AND THEIR USES

Before using any oil, read the Cautions on pages 17–18.

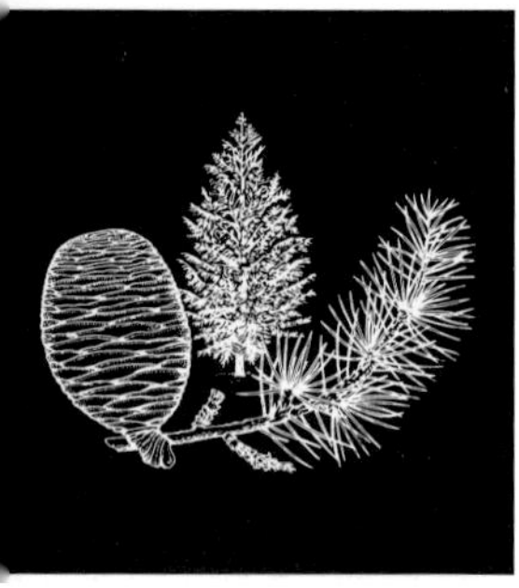

CEDARWOOD

Cedrus atlantica

Character:
CONFIDENT, FIRMLY ROOTED;
SPIRITUAL STRENGTH

Cedarwood (also called Libanol) is distilled from the wood of the cedar tree. It is one of the oldest essential oils, used in North Africa as a perfume and medicine. In Ancient Egypt it was used both for preserving mummies and as a massage oil. In the nineteenth century it was found to have antiseptic properties.

Aroma:
Harmonious, woody, soft.

Properties:
Antiseptic, astringent, diuretic, emollient, fungicide, harmonising, insecticide, sedative, tonic.

Physical conditions:
Eliminatory system: cystitis, relieves burning pain; kidney tonic
Respiratory system: helpful with asthma, bronchitis, catarrh, coughs
Musculoskeletal system: may ease chronic arthritic and rheumatic pains
Nervous system: relaxing and calming
Skin: good for acne, oily skin, irritation
Scalp and hair: dandruff, seborrhoea.

Mental/emotional conditions:
Focuses attention when lacking concentration; for scattered thoughts, day-dreaming, living in the future. Calms anxiety and nervous tension.

Other uses:
Combine with Sandalwood for room fragrance for meditation.

Applications:
Bath. Inhalation. Massage. Room fragrance.

Blends well with:
Sandalwood.

CHAMOMILE

Anthemis nobilis

Character:
SOOTHING YET STRONG

Chamomile oil is distilled from the white flower heads of the Chamomile herb. There are many types of Chamomile, including Roman, German, and Wild or Moroccan Chamomile. Some are anti-inflammatory, containing azulenes or bisabolene. Wild or Moroccan Chamomile has long been used in the medicine of North Africa.

Aroma:
Fresh, herbaceous, tea-like, ardent.

Properties:
Antispasomodic, calming, cicatrisant, comforting, febrifuge, sedative of nervous system, warming.

Physical conditions:
Digestion: colic, colitis, diarrhoea, gastritis, ulcers
Eliminatory system: bedwetting, cystitis, irritable bowel
Hormonal system: decongestant, good for hot flushes
Musculoskeletal system: used for low back pain, rheumatism, sprains
Nervous system: helpful for depression, headaches, insomnia, when feeling fragile.

Mental/emotional conditions:
For the highly strung and perhaps over-enthusiastic; impulsiveness in helping others; living on nerves and straining energies to their limits.

Applications:
Bath. Face oil/lotion. Facial steaming. Footbath. Inhalation. Massage. Room fragrance.

Blends well with:
Geranium, Lavender, Ylang Ylang.

CLARY SAGE

Salvia sclarea

Character:
BENEVOLENT

Clary Sage is distilled from the lilac flowering tops of a biennial herb with large wrinkled leaves, growing in England, Europe, Russia and the USA. It is related to, but different from, the common sage used in cooking. The name *Salvia* derives from the Latin for 'good health' and the word 'clary' meaning 'clear'; the seeds were once used in a remedy to clear particles from the eyes. Clary Sage can have euphoric effects, and from the 16th century was added to beer by some brewers.

Aroma:
Light, spicy, like drying hay.

Properties:
Antidepressant, antiseptic, carminative, deodorant, sedative, tonic. Regulatory and balancing. Strongly sedative, but sometimes with euphoric effects.

Physical conditions:
Hair: encourages growth
**Hormonal system:* regulates hormones, helpful for pre-menstrual tension and painful periods, also frigidity. Encourages labour.
Musculoskeletal system: relieves cramp, muscle spasm
Nervous system: exhaustion; insomnia from over-work; headaches; migraines
Respiratory system: asthma, throat infections
Skin: excessive perspiration
*Use with caution: can cause excessive bleeding.

Mental/emotional conditions:
Particularly indicated for times of change, domestic, occupational and biological, and when having difficulty in adjusting to changes in life.

Other uses:
Aphrodisiac. Restorative when convalescing.

Applications:
Bath. Hair oil/rinse. Massage. Room fragrance.
*Can cause drowsiness; best not used before driving or drinking alcohol.

Blends well with:
Rosemary, Ylang Ylang.

CYPRESS

Cupressus sempervirens

Character:
SOLEMN, FIRM, UPRIGHT, ASTRINGENT

Cypress oil is distilled from the wood of the majestic cypress tree, which grows in Europe, particularly around the Mediterranean. The tree has been venerated since ancient times, and gave its name to the island of Cyprus. It has also been associated with burial grounds since Greek and Roman days, and is traditionally believed to have supplied the wood for Christ's Cross. Known for its astringent properties, the oil is often used today in perfumery, especially men's cosmetics.

Aroma:
Refreshing, woody, spicy.

Properties:
Antiseptic, antispasmodic, astringent, deodorant, toning, vasoconstrictor.

Physical conditions:
Circulation: haemorrhoids, nosebleeds, varicose veins; cellulitis
Eliminatory system: bedwetting; frequent urination; excessive perspiration
Hormonal system: hormone imbalance; PMT; heavy periods; painful periods; menopause
Hair and scalp: dandruff with oily scalp
Musculoskeletal system: cramps, rheumatism
Nervous system: warms coldness in nervous system
Respiratory system: asthma; coughs (bronchitic and dry); influenza
Skin: can benefit mature, oily and sweaty skin. Helps heal wounds.

Mental/emotional conditions:
For fear of what others think; inability to withstand pressure from others of more dominant personality.

Other uses:
Insecticide; deodorant; male toiletry.

Applications:
Bath. Face lotion. Facial steaming. Hair oil/rinse. Inhalation. Room fragrance.

Blends well with:
Frankincense, Grapefruit, Juniper, Lemon.

EUCALYPTUS

Eucalyptus globulus

Character:
HARMONISING, VIGOROUS,
DEEPLY GROUNDED

Eucalyptus, or Blue Gum is one of the most widely used essential oils; a constituent of cold remedies and inhalants, and strongly antiseptic. The oil is distilled from the blue-green leaves of the Eucalyptus tree, which grows to a great height in warm regions. A native of Tasmania, its leaves were used by the Aborginals as a dressing for wounds. It was introduced to Europe in the eighteenth century.

Aroma:
Resinous, camphorous, clear, powerful.

Properties:
Analgesic, anti-rheumatic, antiseptic, decongestant, deodorising, energy balancing, insecticide.

Physical conditions:
Eliminatory system: cystitis; diarrhoea
Musculoskeletal system: muscular aches and pains; rheumatism (combined with Lemon and Juniper); sciatica
Nervous system: neuralgia
Respiratory system: asthma; bronchitis; catarrh; colds; cold with headache; sinusitis
Skin: burns; inflammatory conditions; insect bites; skin eruptions

Mental/emotional conditions:
Cools heated emotions; balances extreme moods, highs and lows occurring for no apparent reason; aids concentration.

Other uses:
Insect repellent.

Applications:
Bath. Inhalation. Massage.

Blends well with:
Cedarwood, Ginger, Marjoram, Rosemary.

FRANKINCENSE

Boswellia carterii

Character:
INSPIRING AND CONTEMPLATIVE, HARMONISING

Frankincense, or Olibanum is distilled from the resin of a small desert tree growing in the Middle East and North Africa. Famous as a birth gift to the infant Jesus, it has had religious and therapeutic uses for centuries. The Ancient Egyptians burned it in religious ceremonies, and also used it in massage and to rejuvenate the skin. Today it is used as an incense in many religions.

Aroma:
Spicy, resinous, balsamic, almost lemony.

Properties:
Antiseptic, calming, cooling, drying, fortifying, revitalising, stimulating, tonic; uplifting.

Physical conditions:
Circulation: haemorrhoids; nosebleeds
Digestive system: indigestion
Eliminatory system: cystitis
Nervous system: chilliness
Respiratory system: asthma; bronchitis; catarrh; congested lungs; shortness of breath
Skin: acne scarring; ageing; cracked; oily; wrinkles.

Mental/emotional conditions:
For over-attachment to the past; burn-out, with no conditions; reserves; depression; exhaustion and mental fatigue; fears; insecurity; nightmares; panic.

Other uses:
Aid to meditation and spiritual development.

Applications:
Bath. Face oil/lotion. Facial steaming. Inhalation. Massage. Room fragrance.

Blends well with:
Cypress, Ginger, Orange, Sandalwood, Tangerine.

GERANIUM

Pelargonium graveolens

Character:
ADAPTABLE; STRONG WHEN PURE, SWEETENS WITH DILUTION

Geranium, or Rose Geranium is distilled from the fragrant leaves of the Pelargonium, a herbaceous plant with pink flowers. The oil is often obtained from France, Madagascar, Morocco and other warm climates. Geranium was once used as a general healing herb for wounds, fractures, cholera, etc. The oil has beneficial effects on most skin conditions and stimulates the lymphatic system. It is widely used in soaps and perfumes. It is one of the balancing oils; harmonising extreme conditions, both physical and emotional.

Aroma:
Sweet, fruity, rose-like.

Properties:
Analgesic, antidepressant, astringent, balancing, diuretic, harmonising, insecticide, tonic, vasoconstrictor.

Physical conditions:
Circulatory system: a tonic, helps relieve fluid retention and lymphatic congestion
Eliminatory system: a tonic for the liver and kidneys
Hormonal system: regulatory, useful for PMT, painful breasts, irregular or heavy periods, menopausal symptoms
Hair and scalp: balances sebum; helps clear headlice
Nervous system: eases neuralgia and fatigue
**Skin:* good for all types of skin conditions including dermatitis, blotches and eczema, and in skin lotion. Effective in mouth and throat infections.
*N.B. May irritate some skins; patch-test first.

Mental/emotional conditions:
Anti-depressant. Quells acute fright, when totally rigid with fear; escalating anxiety when an emergency arises. Balances extreme moods.

Applications:
Bath. Face oil/lotion. Facial steaming. Hair oil/rinse. Inhalation. Massage. Mouthwash. Room fragrance.

Blends well with:
Most oils, particularly Cedarwood, Cypress, Grapefruit, Lavender, Patchouli, Rosemary.

GINGER

Zingiber officinale

Character:
WARM, SHARP, PLEASING, CONFIDENT

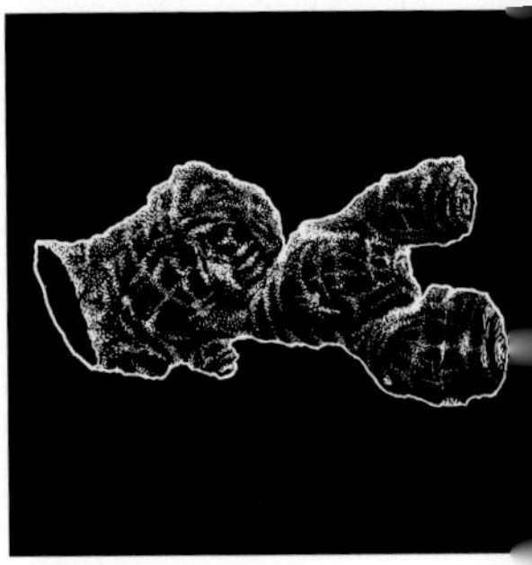

Ginger comes from China, Indonesia and sometimes the West Indies. Ginger is mentioned way back in history, not only in Roman times but also in its ancient home in China. Ginger is well known as a spice or condiment and perhaps its original use was as a food preservative and many people know it as a digestive aid. The ginger herb grows up to 4 feet high or 120 cm, but it is the rhizome which gives the spice an essential oil. The Chinese God of Long Life wore a yellow ginger coloured robe, paying tribute to the use that they saw for the herb. Ginger was introduced into the West Indies by the Spanish to try to steal the trade from the Far East. In fact, very good ginger oil can be obtained from such islands as Jamaica.

Aroma:
Spicy, sharp, warm. Lively and loved.

Properties:
Analgesic, antispasmodic, carminative, expectorant, febrifuge, rubefacient, stimulant, stomachic, sudorific.

Physical conditions:
Digestion: nausea, vomiting, travel sickness, respiratory system. Beneficial for coughs, colds, bronchitis and catarrhal lung conditions. Hormonal system. Promotes menstruation and eases menstrual cramps. Loss of appetite. Flatulence, constipation.
Musculoskeletal system: beneficial in formulations for arthritis, aching muscles and rheumatism.
Nervous system: can be useful for those suffering from stomach migraine.

Mental/emotional conditions:
The essential oil has a fiery character that is very useful for those who need their initiative stimulated or their willpower provoked. It aids in all situations where strength, confidence and determination is required. If procrastination is a problem then ginger will prove very useful. Those who lack confidence or those who have self-doubts that restrain them from actions would do well to use ginger.

Applications:
Massage. Inhalation.
*N.B: Use with caution – do not use undiluted on the skin as it can cause sensitivity.

Blends well with:
Eucalyptus, Frankincense, Lemon, Orange, Patchouli, Sandalwood.

GRAPEFRUIT

Citrus paradisi

Character:
LIGHTNESS AND PURITY

The grapefruit that we know from breakfast times has some obscure origins. It is thought to be a hybrid starting with sweet orange. It probably started life in tropical Asia but we mainly know it these days from its cultivation in the United States, Israel, Cyprus and South Africa. The tree has lovely glossy green leaves and apart from the large yellow fruits has fragrant flowers. In common with other citrus fruits, the essential oil is obtained from the peel of the fruit. Apart from the grapefruit that we know there are also pink grapefruits and some essential oils are tinged that colour. Many years ago, grapefruit was known as Shaddock fruit, named after the sea captain who introduced the fruit to the West Indies, and from there to the United States. Grapefruit essential oil is most commonly used in perfumery and fragrance and occurs in a variety of cosmetics and soaps as well of course as being a food flavouring agent.

Aroma:
Fresh, sweet, citrusy.

Properties:
Anti-depressant, antiseptic, depurative, diuretic, disinfectant, digestive stimulant, lymphatic decongestant.

Physical conditions:
Eliminatory system: lymphatic stimulant with detoxifying and diuretic properties. Cellulitis
Musculoskeletal system: rheumatic pain where swelling is present
Skin: stretch marks. Useful for acne, congested or oily skins
Digestion: sluggish appetite, flatulence, abdominal distension, nausea
Circulation: blood purifier
Nervous system: to relieve feelings of tension, frustration, irritability and moodiness.

Mental/emotional conditions:
Grapefruit is uplifting and reviving and can be used in states of nervous exhaustion and stress particularly when expectations of others are not fulfilled. Grapefruit is the ideal oil for those who comfort eat and for short temper and anger.

Applications:
Face oil. Facial steaming. Massage. Room fragrance.

Blends well with:
Cypress, Geranium, Juniper, Lemon.

JUNIPER

Juniperus communis

Character:
ROUGH, BITTER BUT CONSOLING
STRENGTHENING

Juniper is distilled from the berries or twigs of the juniper tree, a grey-green leafed tree which grows in many parts of the world, thriving in Arctic conditions. Juniper oil has traditionally been used as an antiseptic by many cultures, and in the past was a constituent of herbal medicines for the plague, cholera, typhoid fever and even diabetes. It has also been noted for its reviving qualities, and today is well-known as an ingredient of gin.

Aroma:
Green, herbaceous, refreshing.

Properties:
Antiseptic, anti-rheumatic, antispasmodic, astringent, cleansing, detoxifying, diuretic, insecticide, stimulant, tonic.

Physical conditions:
Circulation: a blood-purifier
Digestive system: generally beneficial; detoxifying, cleanses liver after rich food and too much alcohol
**Eliminatory system:* decongestant and diuretic, good for cystitis, painful urination, kidney problems, cellulitis and fluid retention
Musculoskeletal system: good for arthritis, cramps, rheumatism, sciatica
*N.B. Prolonged use may overstimulate the kidneys. Avoid in cases of serious kidney disease.

Mental/emotional conditions:
Helps to lift guilt, despondency, lack of self-worth; for feeling undeserving of love, and dissatisfied with physical form. Strengthens and supports: good for people in the caring professions.

Other uses:
Hangover; hay fever.

Applications:
Bath. Footbath. Massage. Room fragrance.

Blends well with:
Frankincense, Grapefruit, Rosemary.

LAVENDER

Lavandula angustifolia, hybrida

Character:
MELLOW, PEACEFUL, RELAXING

Lavender oils are distilled from the blue flowering spikes of the lavender bush, just before opening. The plant is widely cultivated in Europe and a hybrid called Lavendin grows wild in the Mediterranean area. The lavender plant has been used in medicine since ancient times, and was introduced to England by the Romans. It has long been known as an antiseptic and an insecticide, and was known for clearing headlice in the 17th century. It is also well known for its skin-healing properties. Lavender oil is invaluable in a home first aid kit, particularly for insect stings, cuts and burns. It is the first choice for insomnia and anxiety, and also boosts the immune system. It is also, of course, a popular constituent of perfumes and cosmetic products.

Aroma:
Clean, balsamic, light, herbaceous.

Properties:
Analgesic, antidepressant, antiseptic, anti-viral, carminative, deodorant, detoxifying, fungicide, insecticide, restorative, sedative. Healing for mind and body.

Physical conditions:
Circulation: relieves chilblains
Eliminatory system: for pain when urinating
Hormonal system: helpful for hot flushes
Hair and scalp: kills headlice; helpful against hair loss
Immune system: stimulates when below par (indicated by chronic or recurrent infections)
Musculoskeletal system: relieves arthritis pain, painful joints and sprains
Nervous system: relaxing and sedative, excellent for insomnia, tension headaches and migraine, and exhaustion
Respiratory system: relieves sore or dry throat
Skin: healing and antiseptic for abscesses, acne, dermatitis, eczema, burns, sunburn, cuts, insect stings and bites

Mental/emotional conditions:
Excellent for all forms of anxiety and tension. For apprehensiveness with vague fears; nightmares and feelings of panic and inner trembling; fear of the dark.

Other uses:
Helpful with tinnitus when sensitive to noise. Counteracts travel sickness.

Applications:
Bath. Face oil/lotion. Facial steaming. Footbath. Hair oil/rinse. Inhalation. Massage. Room fragrance. A drop or two can be dabbed direct on insect stings; use dilute on burns.

Blends well with:
Clary Sage, Eucalyptus, Geranium, Juniper, Patchouli.

LEMON
Citrus limonum

Character:
FRESH, STRONG, VERSATILE.
ADDS CHARACTER; HARMONISES WELL

Lemon oil is pressed from the lemon rind. Several varieties of lemon tree are grown in warm climates; originating in India it was first brought to Europe by the crusaders, and is widely cultivated in Italy. It has long been used as an antiseptic, particularly for bites by disease-carrying insects. Today it is used as a flavouring in foods and drinks.

Aroma:
Fresh, clean, refreshing, lively.

Properties:
Anti-infections, anti-rheumatic, antiseptic, astringent, carminative, detoxifying, diuretic, insecticide, laxative, stimulating, styptic, tonic, refreshing, uplifting. Acts on the physical, mental and spiritual defence systems.

Physical conditions:
Circulation: a good tonic, helps to lower high blood pressure; stems nosebleeds and external bleeding
Digestion: improves digestion, balances acidity
Eliminatory system: helpful for cellulitis and fluid retention; generally cleansing and detoxifying
Hair and scalp: cleanses greasy hair
Immune system: stimulates when below par (indicated by chronic or recurrent infections)
Musculoskeletal system: helps relieve aches and pains
Nervous system: soothes neuralgia
Respiratory system: relieves colds, sore throats, influenza and coughs
Skin: clears corns, warts and verrucas; broken veins; clears skin of dead cells.

Mental/emotional conditions:
Refreshing and clarifying; good for feelings of resentment or bitterness about life's experiences; touchiness; when grudging of others' luck or success.

Applications:
Bath. Face oil/lotion. Facial steaming. Footbath. Hair oil/rinse. Inhalation. Massage. Room fragrance. Apply direct to corns, warts and verrucas.

*N.B. Dilute well as high dosage may irritate skin or cause photosensitivity.

Blends well with:
Chamomile, Eucalyptus, Frankincense, Ginger, Grapefruit, Juniper, Lavender, Sandalwood, Ylang Ylang.

MARJORAM, WOOD OR SPANISH

Thymus mastichina; Majorana sylvestre

Character:
GENTLE, COMFORTING, WARMING

Wood or Spanish Marjoram is distilled from the small, white flowers of the herb which grows in southern Europe and is widely used in flavouring food. The oil is physically and mentally calming and pain-relieving, useful in rheumatic and back pains, and in promoting the circulation.

Aroma:
Warm, herbaceous, with Eucalyptus notes.

Properties:
Analgesic, antiseptic, anti-spasmodic, calming, carminative, digestive, laxative, restorative, sedative, tonic.

Physical conditions:
Digestion: soothing, may help with indigestion, flatulence and constipation
Eliminatory system: a decongestant
Musculoskeletal system: a muscle relaxant; relieves aches and pains, especially when cold and stiff; for stiffness after sport
Nervous system: headaches, migraines, insomnia
Respiratory system: good for bronchitis, chest infections, colds, sinusitis; clears head congestion.

Mental/emotional conditions:
Soothing and relaxing, good when feeling hostile or withdrawn. For those who find it hard to display emotions. Also for mental strain, hyperactivity, irrational thoughts.

Applications:
Bath. Facial steaming. Footbath. Inhalation. Massage. Room fragrance.

Blends well with:
Lavender, Lemon.

ORANGE

Citrus sinensis

Character:
MELLOW, WARMING, SOOTHING, CHEERING

Orange oil is expressed from the zest of the orange fruit; the tree originated in China and today is grown widely in hot climates. It was probably brought to Europe by the Crusaders; later it was taken to California by the early missionaries. The oil is used in perfume and for food flavouring. It works well on the emotions, lifting gloom and depression and encouraging a hopeful outlook.

Aroma:
Mellow, fruity, sweet.

Properties:
Anticoagulant, antidepressant, antiseptic, antispasmodic, carminative, detoxifying, digestive, sedative, tonic.

Physical conditions:
Digestion: calms nervous stomach, dyspepsia, gastric spasm; also helpful for both constipation and diarrhoea
Eliminatory system: helps sweat out toxins from skin
Musculoskeletal system: stimulates body tissue repair, relieves muscular aches and pains
Nervous system: a balancing oil, calming and relaxing as needed; can help insomnia
Respiratory system: good for bronchitis, colds
**Skin:* good for ageing, dry skin, and dermatitis.

Mental/emotional conditions:
Very good for depression, hopelessness, sadness, and lack of joy; energises when apathetic, resigned and unable to make necessary changes. Good during periods of hard work.

Other uses:
Aids absorption of Vitamin C; brings down temperature; energises.

Applications:
Bath. Face oil/lotion. Inhalation. Massage. Room fragrance.

*N.B. Dilute well as high dosage may irritate skin or cause photosensitivity.

Blends well with:
Ginger, Rosemary, Ylang Ylang.

PATCHOULI

Pogostemon cablin

Character:
STRENGTH, EARTHINESS, RICH

Patchouli will be remembered by all those who love the 60's and 70's. Patchouli was common among all the hippie generation. It was also popular in Victorian England because fabrics and shawls imported from India were scented with Patchouli as a form of moth proofing but the buyers just loved the aroma. Today Patchouli mainly comes from Indonesia. Patchouli is actually a small herb and the essential oil is distilled from the dried leaves. The herb can be harvested up to three times a year but the best oil comes from leaves which are actually harvested in the rainy season. Patchouli is also very popular in the perfumers' repertoire. It underpins many oriental type perfumes and is valued not only for its earthy and exotic fragrance but also because it acts as a fixative in perfume materials. This use speaks of its tenacity and strength. The aroma of Patchouli is said to improve with age and Patchouli at its best has a distinctive dry note or feel to it.

Aroma:
Sweet, warm, earthy with a hint of spice. Drier with age.

Properties:
Anti-depressant, antiseptic, aphrodisiac, deodorant, sedative, cicatrisant.

Physical conditions:
Eliminatory system: useful for fluid retention and where diuretic properties are required; cellulite. It has special deodorising effects
Skin: as a tissue regenerator – especially good for cracked, rough or sore skin, useful against acne, eczema and similar skin conditions
Hair: a general tonic for scalp disorders
Circulation: in combination with other oils such as citrus it is useful as a vascular decongestant and suitable for varicose veins.

Mental/emotional conditions:
Patchouli is said to be grounding and integrating. It's useful for anyone who feels outside reality. It can be helpful to anyone who feels overactive and has quietening and relaxing effects. Similarly it can be helpful for those suffering from sexual anxiety, frigidity or impotence. For those shattered by work it can be a rest and relaxation bringing people back to being in touch with themselves.

Other uses:
Patchouli has been used as a meditation aid and for providing inspiration.

Applications:
Face oil/lotion. Facial steaming. Massage. Room fragrance. Bathing.

Blends well with:
Geranium, Ginger, Lavender, Rosewood, Sandalwood, Ylang, Ylang.

PEPPERMINT
Mentha piperita

Character:
HOT AND COLD; STIMULATING

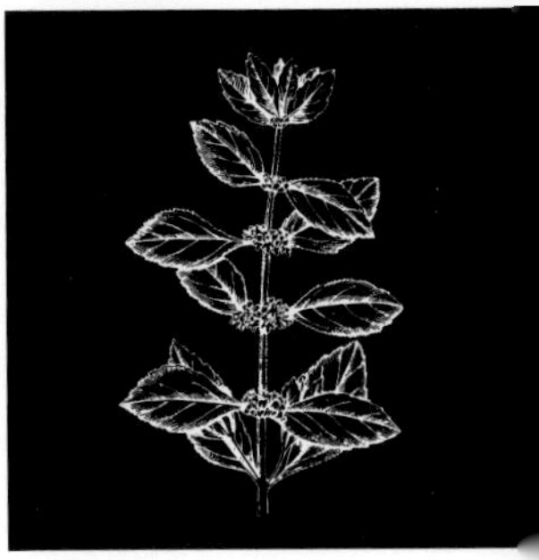

Peppermint is distilled from the whole herb, an invasive herbaceous plant. There are many species, including Mint and Spearmint, all of which are used widely in medicines and in flavouring confectionery, toothpaste, etc. In Greek mythology, Mentha was a nymph, who was pursued by Pluto, the god of the underworld. His jealous wife trod her into the ground, but Pluto ensured her survival by transforming her into the herb. Peppermint has been used for centuries for digestive problems; in warm climates peppermint tea is commonly drunk after meals. The oil is also good for aches and pains, and respiratory congestion. It is rich in menthol, often used in embrocations and inhalants. While best known for digestive and respiratory conditions, it has other lesser known but very useful applications.

Aroma:
Minty, fresh, slightly sweet, powerful.

Properties:
Anti-inflammatory, analgesic, antiseptic, antispasmodic, astringent, carminative, clarifying, cooling, detoxifying, deodorising, pain-relieving, refreshing, stimulating, vasoconstrictor.

Physical conditions:
Digestion: useful for bad breath, colic, constipation, diarrhoea, flatulence, food poisoning, gastritis, indigestion, nausea, nervous dyspepsia, vomiting
Eliminatory system: irritable bowel; encourages perspiration
Musculoskeletal system: anti-inflammatory for muscle aches and pains. Excellent for aching feet
Nervous system: pain-relieving, eases headaches, migraines
Respiratory system: clearing for colds, flu and sinus congestion, laryngitis
Skin: cooling for inflammation, sunburn, irritation; can help dermatitis and ringworm. Balances greasy skin, helps remove blackheads.

Mental/emotional conditions:
For shyness and hypersensitivity to many things; for those dominated by strong likes and dislikes.

Other uses:
Travel sickness, shock, faintness, vertigo.

Applications:
Bath. Face oil/lotion. Facial steaming. Footbath. Hair oil/rinse. Inhalation. Massage. Mouthwash. Room fragrance.

*N.B. Use with caution and dilute well, as this oil is extremely powerful and could cause irritation of skin and mucous membranes.

Blends well with:
Best left alone as it overwhelms other essences.

ROSEMARY

Rosmarinus officinalis

Character:
VIGOROUS, PENETRATING, STIMULATING

Rosemary is distilled from the needle-like leaves of the evergreen bush, which is also a popular kitchen herb. Originating in Asia, rosemary now grows in Europe, particularly the south, and is cultivated for oil in France and Tunisia. Its Latin name Rosmarinus means 'sea-dew'. Rosemary was sacred to the ancient Greeks and Romans who used it in incense and as a symbol of regeneration; in 14th-century Europe it was believed to have rejuvenating powers and was an ingredient of Hungary Water, a very popular toilet water. Rosemary oil is known as a blood and lymph stimulant; since it stimulates the local blood supply it is excellent for aches and pains. It has also long been valued as a brain stimulant; the ancient Romans wore rosemary sprigs behind the ear to aid concentration and memory. It has also been used with some success to treat baldness and falling hair; while it may not affect all cases, it is certainly worth trying.

Aroma:
Strong, woody, camphoraceous, refreshing.

Properties:
Analgesic, antidepressant, anti-rheumatic, antiseptic, antispasmodic, astringent, carminative, cleansing, clearing, digestive, diuretic, invigorating, stimulating, tonic.

Physical conditions:
**Circulation:* boosts circulation, heart tonic and stimulant, normalises low blood pressure. Relieves chilblains and chilliness
Digestion: stimulates digestive process
Eliminatory system: boosts liver and kidney function; good for constipation, cystitis – and hangovers
Hormonal system: may relieve menstrual pain and fluid retention
Hair and scalp: excellent tonic, may be helpful for baldness and falling hair; good for dandruff and oily scalp
Musculoskeletal system: very useful for aches, pains, sprains, muscle fatigue, and rheumatism
Nervous system: clears headaches, mental fatigue, migraine; stimulates brain and memory
Skin: good for oily skin; boosts circulation.

Mental/emotional conditions:
Clearing and stimulating for feelings of disorientation, indecision and lethargy; feelings of inadequacy; feeling overwhelmed by responsibilities.

Applications:
Bath. Face oil/lotion. Facial steaming. Footbath. Hair oil/rinse. Inhalation. Massage. Room fragrance.
*N.B. Use with caution if suffering from high blood pressure, hypertension, and/or insomnia, or epilepsy.

Blends well with:
Cedarwood, Frankincense, Geranium, Juniper, Orange, Tangerine.

ROSEWOOD
Aniba parviflora

Character:
SOFT SWEETNESS WITH BODY,
BALANCING

Rosewood, or Bois de Rose is distilled from the wood of a South American tree. Its main uses are psychological; it has a balancing effect, uplifting when lethargic and overburdened, soothing anxiety, irritability and inner tension. It is believed to be beneficial to mature skin as a cell stimulant and tissue regenerator and can be helpful with problems of ageing.

Aroma:
Floral with spicy undertones.

Properties:
Antiseptic, antidepressant, aphrodisiac, balancing, calming, deodorant, grounding, regenerative, stabilising, stimulating, uplifting

Physical conditions:
Digestion: nausea with anxiety
Eliminatory system: deodorant
Hormonal system: may be helpful for loss of libido, frigidity, impotence
Immune system: boosts body's defence system; helpful for chronic complaints
Nervous system: balancing and stabilising; neurotic; sedative; may relieve headaches accompanied by nausea
Respiratory system: good for throat infections
Skin: cell and tissue stimulant, rejuvenating for dry skin, and ageing skin pigmentation. Relieves insect bites.

Mental/emotional conditions:
Good for rigid attitudes, when over-critical of others, lacking empathy, unyielding to others or to circumstances; for inner tension and rigidity.

Other uses:
Aphrodisiac. Insect repellent.

Applications:
Face oil/lotion. Footbath. Massage. Room fragrance.

Blends well with:
Cedarwood, Frankincense, Geranium, Patchouli, Rosemary, Tangerine, Ylang Ylang.

SANDALWOOD

Santalum album

Character:
PERSISTENT, SENSUOUS

Sandalwood, or Bois de Santal is distilled from the heartwood of an evergreen Indian tree which is parasitic on other trees. Sandalwood has been popular for centuries in furniture and casket making, as well as incense, and was used to build Indian temples. The ancient Egyptians used Sandalwood oil in embalming and medicines. It is valued as incense today in India, China and Japan. In India it has strong spiritual connotations, being burned at weddings and funerals; it is also used medicinally for genito-urinary problems. Believed to encourage self-expression, Sandalwood is very helpful for laryngitis and sore throats. It is exceptionally long-lasting, and is used as a fixative in perfumes.

Aroma:
Warm, rich, sweet, woody.

Properties:
Antiseptic, antispasmodic, aphrodisiac, astringent, carminative, diuretic, healing, regenerative, relaxing, soothing, tonic.

Physical conditions:
Eliminatory system: alleviates cystitis; lymphatic decongestant
Hormonal system: a sensual stimulant, it can be helpful with sexual problems
Immune system: boosts immune deficiency, characterised by persistent infections
Nervous system: very relaxing for nervous tension
Respiratory system: useful for laryngitis, chest, throat and lung infections, bronchitic and dry cough
Skin: good for ageing, dry skins; relieves itching, inflammation and dry eczema. Antiseptic for acne, boils, cuts and wounds.

Mental/emotional conditions:
Balancing for people who are possessive and manipulative, who like their own way; for difficulty in forgiving; for those who do things for others but fear a lack of return. Helpful with obsessional attitudes, worry about past and future, feeling unsupported. Brings peace and acceptance. May be helpful for sexual anxiety.

Other uses:
An aid to meditation, and spiritual development, associated with the 'third eye' and development of intuition.

Applications:
Bath. Face oil/lotion. Facial steaming. Inhalation. Massage. Room fragrance.

Blends well with:
Cypress, Frankincense, Ginger, Lavender, Lemon, Patchouli, Ylang Ylang.

TANGERINE OR MANDARIN
(Citrus reticulata)

Character:
REFINED, SOFT, CHEERFUL,
UPLIFTING, SWEET

Tangerine or Mandarin oil is expressed from the zest of the citrus fruit, which originated in China and is now cultivated in other warm climates, including the USA and Sicily. Tangerine and Mandarin trees come from the same botanical source. Tangerine oil is a yellow-gold colour, with a light-blue fluorescence in the best quality oils (quality depends on the time of the harvest). Like many oils, Tangerine can be both relaxing and tonic, according to needs. Its medicinal properties are similar to those of Orange.

Aroma:
Sweet, fruity, tangy.

Properties:
Antiseptic, antispasmodic, cheering, sedative, soothing, stomachic, tonic, unwinding, uplifting.

Physical conditions:
Carsiovascular system: calms excitation and cardiovascular erethism which often goes with indigestion
Circulation: tonifies the peripheral circulation in the extremities; revives tired and aching limbs
Digestion: a digestive tonic, good for gastric complaints including constipation, diarrhoea and flatulence; stimulates bile excretion, thereby activating the stomach and liver
Nervous system: sedative, hypnotic; soothes and relaxes; good for insomnia
Skin: a useful skin tonic, encouraging circulation.

Mental/emotional conditions:
Good for dejection, depression, emotional emptiness; regrets for ageing and loss of the past; feeling watered down.

Other uses:
Cheering and uplifting; popular as a room fragrance in hospices.

Applications:
Bath. Face oil/lotion. Footbath. Massage. Room fragrance.

Blends well with:
Chamomile, Clary Sage, Geranium, Lavender, Lemon.

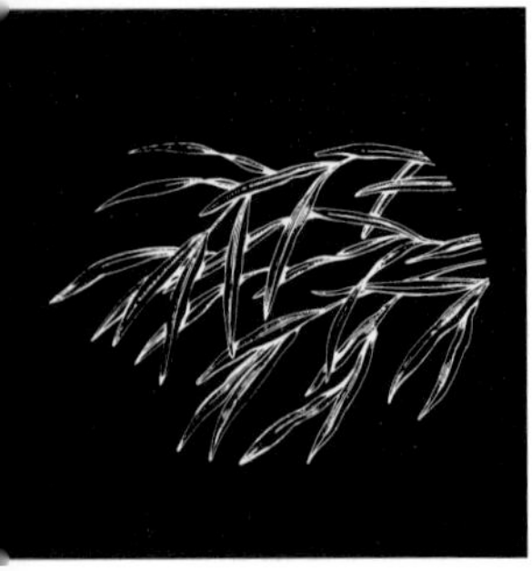

TEA TREE

Melaleuca alternifolia

Character:
VIGOROUS, REVITALISING, REGENERATING

Tea Tree oil is distilled from the leaves and branches of the Tea Tree, a small tree belonging to the myrtle family, and a native of the marshland of New South Wales. It acquired its name when Captain Cook's sailors used it to brew up a substitute for tea. Tea Tree oil is a powerful antiseptic and fungicide and boosts the depleted immune system. Its wide range of medicinal uses have been verified by research. In the 1920s and '30s, laboratory research in Australia confirmed that it was not only a very strong antiseptic but non-toxic and non-irritant. A report noted that it dissolved pus, leaving infected wounds clean. During World War II it was issued in army tropical first aid kits, but the development of antibiotics led to a decline in its use. A 1972 study showed that Tea Tree oil was effective in many foot problems, including athlete's foot, corns, bunions and other fungal infections. It has also been used by practitioners to treat ringworm and thrush and more recently it has been found helpful with Candida albicans and chronic cystitis. It is an ideal first aid home remedy; for serious chronic conditions readers should consult a qualified practitioner.

Aroma:
Medicinal, penetrating.

Properties:
Powerful antiseptic, anti-viral, bactericide, cleansing, detoxifying, fungicide, insecticide, purifying, stimulating.

Physical conditions:
Eliminatory system: used to treat urinary infections, cystitis and Candida
Hair and scalp: impetigo, headlice; dry scalp and dandruff
Immune system: activates the white blood cells to fight infection
Respiratory system: combats infections of the throat, lungs and ears; bad breath
Skin: very cleansing; antiseptic for acne, boils, cuts, wounds, bites; effective with corns, warts, verrucas; fights fungal infections (e.g. athlete's foot, ringworm) soothes and heals irritating/itchy conditions – chicken pox rash, psoriasis, impetigo, nappy rash, genital itching, pruritis; treatment for mouth ulcers, and mouth/gum infections

Mental/emotional conditions:
Refreshing and revitalising; for feelings of uncleanness; for over-preoccupation with detail.

Applications:
Bath. Face oil/lotion. Facial steaming. Footbath. Hair oil/rinse. Inhalation. Massage. Mouthwash. Room fragrance.

Blends well with:
Best used alone.

YLANG YLANG
Cananga odorata

Character:
VOLUPTUOUS, SENSUAL, EXOTIC, YET REASSURING

Ylang Ylang, 'The Flower of Flowers' is distilled from the yellow flowers of a tree growing in Indonesia, the Philippines and Madagascar. It is also known as the 'perfume tree'. In the South Seas women combine the oil with coconut oil to dress their hair, and in Indonesia the blossoms are spread on the beds of honeymoon couples. The oil is used in expensive perfumes. While Ylang Ylang has physical properties, its main effects are on the emotions, and it is known as an aphrodisiac. It is also reassuring and confidence-building.

Aroma:
Heavy, sweetly narcotic, floral.

Properties:
Antidepressant, aphrodisiac, calming, euphoric, sensual, sedative, uplifting.

Physical conditions:
Circulation: calming for tachycardia, reduces high blood pressure; regulates adrenaline flow
Hormonal system: balances the hormones; a uterine tonic. May help keep breasts firm. Helpful for sexual problems
Hair and scalp: tonic, promotes hair growth
Nervous system: has relaxing effect
Skin: balances both dry and oily skins.

Mental/emotional conditions:
Calms anger, fear, frustration, irritability. Is believed to act on the emotional heart centre, healing feelings of guilt, jealousy, resentment and selfishness. Also helpful in times of change.

Applications:
Bath. Face oil/lotion. Hair oil/rinse. Massage. Room fragrance.

Blends well with:
Clary Sage, Geranium, Lavender, Lemon, Orange, Patchouli.

FURTHER READING

Aromatherapy: An A–Z
Patricia Davis, C.W. Daniel & Co. Ltd., 1999

Aromatherapy: A Guide for Home Use
Christine Westwood, Amberwood Publishing Ltd., 1991

Aromatherapy For Women
Maggie Tisserand, Thorsons Publishers Ltd., 1999

Aromatherapy: Massage with Essential Oils
Christine Wildwood, Element, 1991

The Book of Massage
Linda Lidell, Ebury Press, 1991

The Complete Book of Massage
Clare Maxwell-Hudson, Dorling-Kindersley, 1988

The Directory of Essential Oils
Wanda Sellar, C.W. Daniel & Co., 1994

Practical Aromatherapy: How to use Essential Oils to Restore Vitality
Shirley Price, Thorsons Publishing Group, 1994

The Practice of Aromatherapy
Jean Valnet, C.W. Daniel & Co., 1980

WHERE TO FIND AN AROMATHERAPIST

The following organisations will supply lists of qualified Aromatherapists. Please enclose stamped addressed envelopes with your enquiries.

The International Federation of Aromatherapists
Stamford House, 214 Chiswick High Road, London W4 1TH, UK

The Register of Qualified Aromatherapists
PO Box 3431, Danbury, Chelmsford, Essex CM3 4UA, UK

The Aromatherapy Organisations Council
PO Box 19834, London SE25 6WF, UK